I SPY

SCHOOL DAYS

A BOOK OF
PICTURE
RIDDLES

Photographs by Walter Wick

Riddles by Jean Marzollo

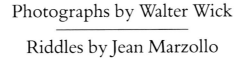

Cartwheel
·B·O·O·K·S·®

SCHOLASTIC INC.

New York   Toronto   London   Auckland   Sydney
Mexico City   New Delhi   Hong Kong   Buenos Aires

For my nieces, Heather, Jessica, and Emily,
and my nephews, David, Peter, and Michael

———

W. W.

For Marjorie Holderman, Joanne Marien, and Gerrie Paige

———

J.M.

I SPY: A BOOK OF PICTURE RIDDLES

*New York Public Library: One Hundred Titles — For Reading and Sharing;
California Children's Media Award, Honorable Mention*

I SPY CHRISTMAS: A BOOK OF PICTURE RIDDLES

Publishers Weekly, starred review; Parents Magazine, Best Books List

I SPY FUN HOUSE: A BOOK OF PICTURE RIDDLES

*Publishers Weekly, starred review; Publishers Weekly, Best Books of 1993;
American Bookseller Pick of the Lists*

I SPY MYSTERY: A BOOK OF PICTURE RIDDLES

*Publishers Weekly, starred review; Publishers Weekly, Best Books of 1993;
American Bookseller Pick of the Lists; National Parenting Publications Award,
Honorable Mention*

I SPY FANTASY: A BOOK OF PICTURE RIDDLES

Book design by Carol Devine Carson

Text copyright © 1995 by Jean Marzollo.
Photographs copyright © 1995 by Walter Wick.
All rights reserved. Published by Scholastic Inc.

CARTWHEEL BOOKS and the CARTWHEEL BOOKS logo are registered trademarks of Scholastic Inc.
I SPY is a trademark of Scholastic Inc.
No part of this publication may be reproduced in whole or in part, or
stored in a retrieval system, or transmitted in any form or by any
means, electronic, mechanical, photocopying, recording, or other-
wise, without written permission of the publisher. For information
regarding permission, write to Scholastic Inc., 557 Broadway,
New York, NY 10012.

Library of Congress Cataloging-in-Publication Data

Wick, Walter.
   I spy school days: a book of picture riddles / photographs by
Walter Wick; riddles by Jean Marzollo.
       p.   cm.
   "I spy books"
   ISBN 0-590-48135-5
   1. Picture puzzles — Juvenile literature.   [1. Picture puzzles.]
   I. Marzollo, Jean.   II. Title.
   GV1507.P47W528   1995
   793.3 — dc20   94-43629

40 39 38 37   07 08

Printed in Singapore   46

First Scholastic printing, September 1995

TABLE OF CONTENTS

Picture riddles fill this book;
Turn the pages! Take a look!

Use your mind, use your eye;
Read the riddles — play I SPY!

I spy a magnet, a monkey, a mouse,
A squash, two flags, five 4's, a house;

A bird on a B, an exit sign,
A UFO, and a valentine.

9

I spy a rabbit, a rhyming snake,
An apple, a shark, and a birthday cake;

An unfinished word, a whale, two dimes,
Tic-tac-toe, and JUAN three times.

I spy an acorn, a cricket, a 3,
A shell in a nest, a shell from the sea;

Three feathers, two frogs, a ladybug, too,
Ten drops of water, and thread that is blue.

I spy a frog, a checkerboard 3,
A zigzag 4, and a zebra Z;

A rabbit, an arrow, a girl named DOT,
Six red blocks, and the missing knot.

I spy a marble, a clothespin clamp,
FUN, two keys, and a ruler ramp;

Three helmets, a hand, a hammer, a heart,
A checker, a chair, and a chalkboard chart.

I spy a schoolhouse, three camels, a bell,
A lighthouse, a swan, and a basket that fell;

A paintbrush, a drum, an upside-down block,
A calendar card, and a grandfather clock.

I spy a mail truck, a valentine cart,
A blue eyeball I, and a five-button heart;

Six arrows, two horses, two airplanes, two clocks,
A key, and a card that is in the wrong box.

I spy a chimney, an anthill, a four,
A face with a smile, a star, and a score;

A feather, a twig, three footprints, a key,
A boat, two birds, a button, and BE.

The Stegosaurus ate plants for food.

Bobby C.

Stegosaurus walks on four legs and is my favorite dinosaur.

Rosa

Nobody knows what they are really like because they only have the bones.

This shows how big a stegosaurus is compared to a school bus.

Joel

Stegosaurus brain was only as big as a walnut.

Stegosaurus' tail spikes could

I spy a walnut, two turtles, a pail,
Two eggs that are hatching, a clothespin, a snail;

Brian J.
I like the stegasaurus because it has spikes on its tail.
carrie
Stegosaurus babies were hatched from eggs like reptiles.
CANADA
Wyoming
Utah
Colorado
Oklahoma
Mexico
Stars show where Stegosduruses were found. Toby
A Dinosaur Dig
Fossils show what the bones were like. Paleontologists are the people who like to dig them out of the rocks and study them.
Roberto
long as a yard stick.
Book of Dinosaur FACTS

Ten pinecones, an ant, a shovel, a plane,
A little red star, three frogs, and a chain.

I spy a kick ball, three ladders, and CLOCKS,
A small piece of chalk, four half-circle blocks;

A limo, a phone, and a rolling pin,
A flame, eight stars, and DEW DROP INN.

I spy three carrots, a magical hen,
Four keys, a candle, a cat, and a ten;

A teapot, a tin man, a rabbit asleep,
Anansi the Spider, and Little Bo Peep.

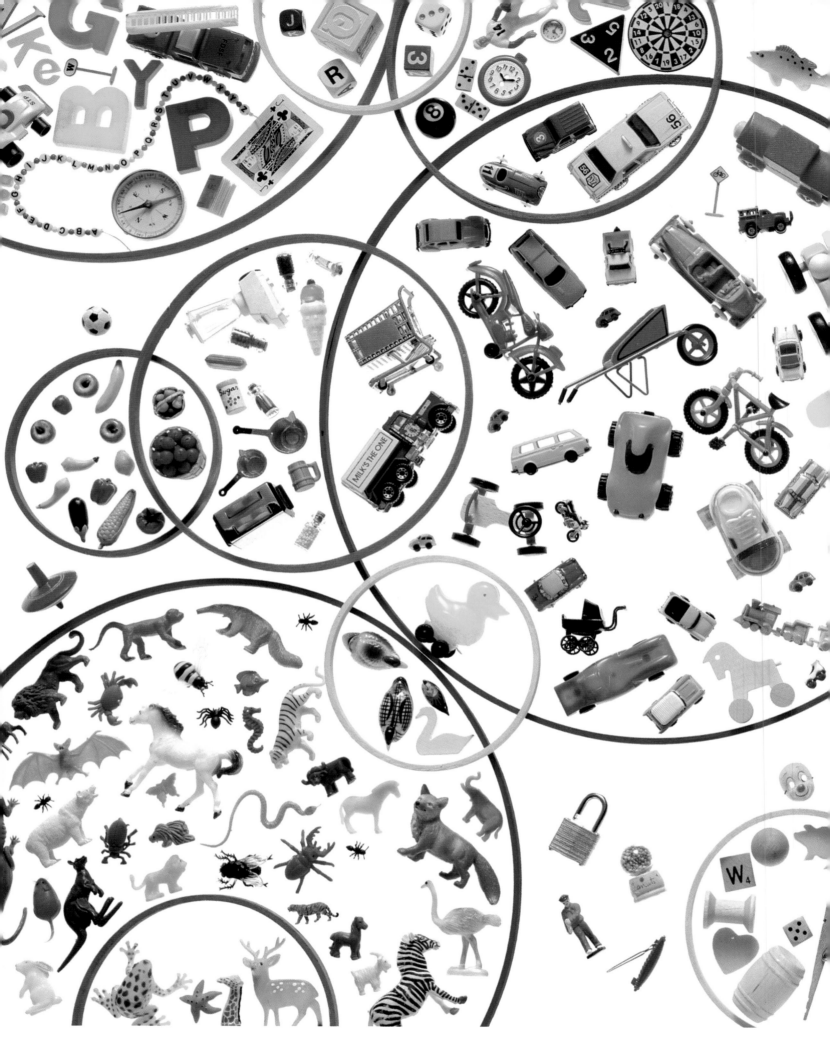

I spy a blender, a duck on a roll,
A pig, four bats, and a fishing pole;

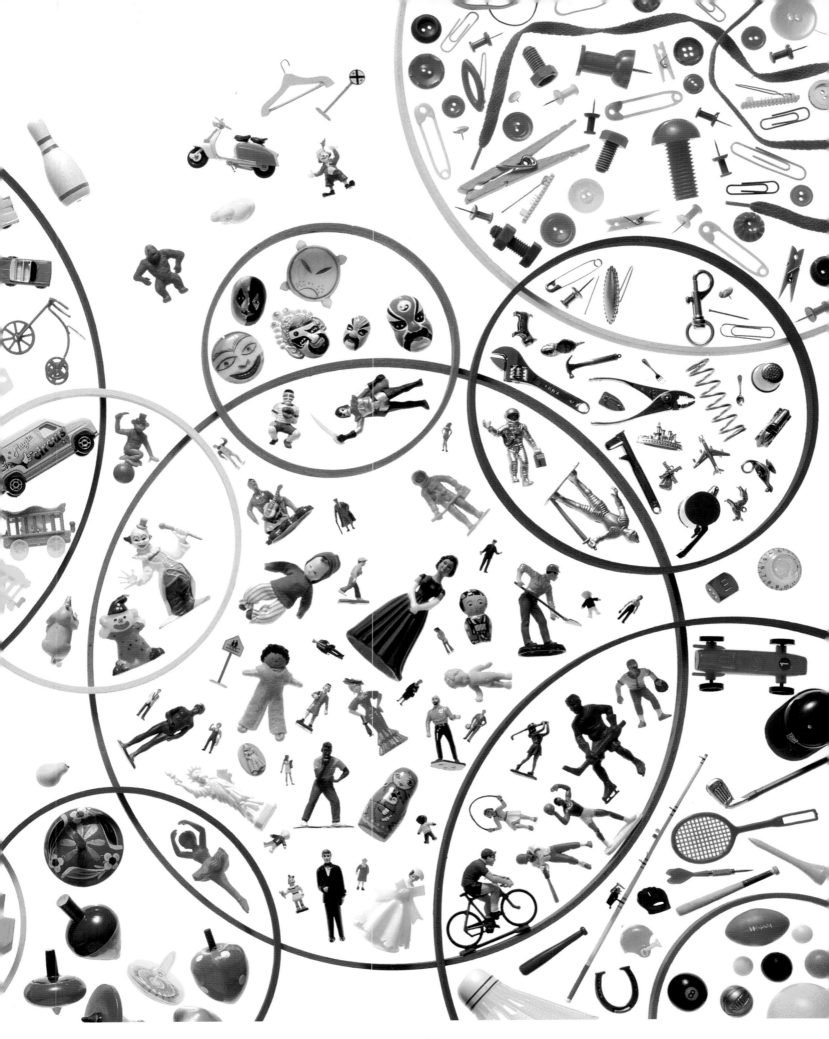

Five barrettes and five yellow rings,
And places for all of the outside things.

I spy a spider, an ice skate, a rake,
Two bracelets that match, a trumpet, a cake;

A dime, the Big Dipper, three flowerpots,
A coat with four buttons, and ten paper dots.

EXTRA CREDIT RIDDLES

"Find Me" Riddle

I'm yellow; I buzz. If you look, you will see.

I'm in every picture. I'm a busy little _____ .

Find the Pictures That Go with These Riddles:

I spy a ruler, a hanger, a wrench,

Eight traffic cones, and an empty bench.

I spy Rapunzel, a small piece of cheese,

A boy in a well, a bed, and some Z's.

I spy a starfish, a paper-clip chain,

A cow, seven hearts, and a yellow jet plane.

I spy a school bus, a camel, a lamp,

Two question marks, and a seven-cent stamp.

I spy a sea horse, a spotted cow,

Three butterflies, and the cat's MEOW.

I spy scissors and three striped cats,
Three pen points, and two yellow hats.

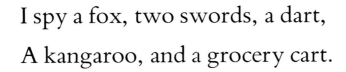

I spy a penny, a thumbtack that's red,
Two black ants, and a gray arrowhead.

I spy a fox, two swords, a dart,
A kangaroo, and a grocery cart.

I spy a feather and two equal signs,
A piece of pie, and three dotted lines.

I spy a truck, a shovel, a J,
Eight rubber bands, and some orange clay.

I spy a shovel, two rabbits, a yak,
A nickel, a knight, and a purple jack.

I spy a starfish, an uppercase I,
A pencil, a snake, and a dragonfly.

I spy a car and a speckled stone,
A chain, a seed, and a small pinecone.

Write Your Own Picture Riddles

There are many more hidden objects and many more possibilities for riddles in this book. Write some rhyming picture riddles yourself, and try them out with friends.

The Story of *I Spy School Days*

After visiting a number of schools where children and staff were successfully pursuing their own *I Spy* writing and art projects, Jean Marzollo and Walter Wick decided to create *I Spy School Days*. In order to celebrate the joy of intellectual discovery, the book has self-motivating and self-rewarding learning activities imbedded in the photographs. For example, when children look at the balloon-popper picture, "Levers, Ramps, and Pulleys," can they predict what will happen when the ball rolls down the chute? (By the way, after many trial runs, the balloon popper finally worked. Walter Wick made a video, recording the event.) When children study the picture called "Sorting and Classifying," they will discover that the circles contain different categories of things, but what will they deduce about the places where the circles overlap? How will they describe those sets?

Inspired by the eagerness of children to solve creative and intellectual problems, even at the youngest levels, Jean Marzollo and Walter Wick hope that *I Spy School Days* will inspire readers to be ever more curious, think logically, observe carefully, read and write interesting words, share ideas, work cooperatively, take risks, and make beautiful things.

Jean Marzollo and Walter Wick together conceived the ideas for the photographs in *I Spy School Days*. Then Walter Wick created all the sets for *I Spy School Days* in his studio, photographing them with an 8″ by 10″ view camera. As much as possible, he used ordinary classroom materials and familiar

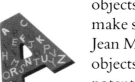

objects from the environment so that readers who desire to make similar projects can do so. As the sets were constructed, Jean Marzollo and Walter Wick conferred by phone and fax on objects to go in the sets, selecting things for their rhyming potential, as well as their aesthetic, playful, and educational qualities. The final riddles were written upon completion of the photographs.

Walter Wick, the inventor of many photographic games for *Games* magazine, is the photographer of *I Spy: A Book of Picture Riddles*, *I Spy Christmas*, *I Spy Fun House*, *I Spy Mystery*, and *I Spy Fantasy*. He is also a freelance photographer with credits including over 300 magazine and book covers, including *Newsweek*, *Discover*, *Psychology Today*, and Scholastic's *Let's Find Out* and *SuperScience*. Mr. Wick graduated from the Paier Art School in New Haven, Connecticut. This is his sixth book for Scholastic.

Jean Marzollo, a graduate of the Harvard Graduate School of Education, has written many children's books, including the *I Spy* books, *In 1492*, *In 1776*, *Ten Cats Have Hats*, *Sun Song*, *Pretend You're a Cat*, and *Close Your Eyes*. She is also the author of *My First Book of Biographies* and *Happy Birthday, Martin Luther King*. **Carol Devine Carson**, the book designer for the *I Spy* series, is an art director for a major publishing house in New York City. For nineteen years, Marzollo and Carson produced Scholastic's kindergarten magazine, *Let's Find Out*.

Acknowledgments

Again, we are grateful for the support and assistance of Grace Maccarone, Bernette Ford, Edie Weinberg, and many others at Scholastic. We also very much appreciate the help of Molly Friedrich at Aaron Priest Agency, Linda Cheverton-Wick, Elizabeth Woodson, Tina Chaden, Barbara Ardizone, Maria McGowan, Bruce Morozko, Frank and Ray Hills, Denis Gouey, Gator Laplante, and Lee Hitt. To Kevin Williams we extend a special thanks for his valuable and patient assistance throughout the entire *I Spy School Days* project.

Walter Wick and Jean Marzollo